Willie and Bo at the Party

A Funny Laundry Day

WRITTEN BY

MARGARET CARDENAS

ILLUSTRATED BY

KENNY ESTRELLA

Olumpus Story House
www.olympusstoryhouse.com

CONTENTS

Willie and Bo at the Party

Willie and Bo are excited because the yard is filled with kids.
They are all running, and playing dodge ball and jump rope, and
climbing trees, or chasing Willie and Bo.

There are a lot of adults, too. Some of the men are playing horse shoes. Some of the men are barbecuing. The women are inside finishing the cakes and salads and beans.

Everyone is busy and having fun. The kids are happy to be together, and happy to be at Ma and Pa's with Willie and Bo. Willie likes for Christian to feed him tortillas and to rub his beard. The other kids want a turn feeding Willie, too.

Abigail and Hattie try to keep the ball away from Bo by throwing it over his head to each other. But Bo finally jumped high and caught it.

Bo is running away with the ball and some of
the kids chase him to get it back.

Soon Ma and the ladies are putting food on the tables on the patio. There is a lot of food! The men bring the hot dogs and hamburgers. Ma put three cakes on the food table.

Soon Pa calls everyone to come and eat. Ma tells Willie and
Bo to go play alone for a while. Everyone eats and has a
good time together.

Next we all sing Happy Birthday to Pa. Then Ma serves the cake. When the kids are through eating they go off to play again.

When everyone else finishes eating they leave the tables to watch Pa open his birthday presents. All the messy plates are still on the table, but Ma will clean up in a little while.

When Ma came back to dean up she saw Willie and Bo at the tables eating the food from the plates. How silly! Willie and Bo wanted a party, too!

A Funny
Laundry Day

Today is washday, so Ma is washing sheets and towels.

It is a beautiful day. It is warm and sunny, so Ma
hung the clothes outside to dry.

Hattie and Lucy came over to help Ma work in the garden.

They pulled weeds and gave them to Willie.
Willie likes to eat weeds.

Hattie and Lucy got tired of working in the garden, so they went inside the house with Ma for cookies and milk.

After a while the girls heard Bo barking outside. Hattie looked
out the window and said Bo was chasing a ghost.

Ma and Lucy hurried to the window to look, and Bo was chasing something white that was running across the yard.

Hattie and Lucy followed Ma outside to see what the ghost could be. Ma said, "Look! It's Willie!" Willie and Bo had been running and playing under the sheets hanging outside, and one got caught on Willie.

Hattie and Lucy laughed at Willie and Bo, and ran to chase them.

The girls caught Willie and took the sheet off him.
Silly Willie! It's not Halloween!